The New Quilt 2

The New Quilt 2

Dairy Barn: Quilt National

The Taunton Press

Front cover: detail of *Bird's Paradise* by Dorle
Stern-Straeter (the full piece is shown on p. 4).
Back cover: detail of *Peace Links at the End of the
Rainbow* by Catherine McConnell Stanton (the
full piece is shown on p. 72). Photographs:
Brian Blauser.

The artists retain copyright to the individual
works shown in this book.

Taunton
BOOKS & VIDEOS

for fellow enthusiasts

© 1993 by The Taunton Press, Inc.
All rights reserved.

First printing: May 1993
Printed in the United States of America

ISBN: 1-56158-056-2
ISSN: 1068-7270

A THREADS Book

THREADS ® is a trademark of The Taunton Press, Inc.,
registered in the U.S. Patent and Trademark Office.

The Taunton Press, 63 South Main Street, Box 5506,
Newtown, CT 06470-5506

Acknowledgments

The staff and Board of Trustees of the Dairy Barn Cultural Arts Center are proud to present Quilt National '93, unquestionably the most powerful and sophisticated quilt show yet.

It's one thing to come up with an idea such as Quilt National, it's quite another to keep it going 15 years down the line. And not only is Quilt National still going, but also it has grown and matured beyond anyone's expectations. That has meant a lot of work, support and dedication on the part of many different individuals and groups whom we wish to acknowledge.

We will always be grateful for the vision that Nancy Crow, Harriet Anderson, Virginia Randles, Françoise Barnes and others had when they put together the first Quilt National in 1979, almost before the paint was dry on the newly dedicated Dairy Barn Arts Center. That show made art history and brought the attention of artists, art critics, museums, galleries and art lovers around the world to the Dairy Barn and the "new" quilt.

We applaud the insight and efforts of the three jurors, Elizabeth Busch, Michael Monroe and Judi Warren, who selected this outstanding collection of quilts from a field of 1,100.

We also feel especially thankful for the financial and in-kind support over the past 15 years that has helped us weather some of the most challenging financial times for arts organizations. It has enabled us to produce, through thick and thin, the highest quality art-quilt shows in the world. Special thanks go to those who contributed not only to Quilt National '93 but also to past Quilt Nationals: the Athens County Convention and Visitors Bureau, the City of Athens, Fairfield Processing Corporation (makers of Poly-fil® brand fiber products) and the Ohio Arts Council. This year, we welcome our new sponsor, Friends of Fiber Art International.

We cannot fully measure all the help we've received from volunteers in this and past Quilt Nationals. They've given thousands of hours of help with every detail of the exhibition, from assisting the jurors to packing up the last quilt.

It's difficult to imagine a Quilt National without the talent and expertise of Hilary Fletcher, the Project Director. As we celebrate her tenth anniversary with Quilt National, we recognize the standards of excellence that she has brought to the entire production of this exhibition and to the development of the Dairy Barn Touring Exhibits Program.

And, of course, we thank the Quilt National artists, whose superb works are changing the face of art.

—*Emilie Ezell, Executive Director*

Introduction

n 1979, when the first Quilt National was conceived, the group of artists who organized it and the founders of the Dairy Barn Cultural Arts Center knew that the new quilts emerging from a select group of international artists represented an art form that would remain to evolve and mature. A growing number of artists were "painting" with thread and cloth, but no forum other than mixed-media exhibitions existed to showcase the considerable talent emerging in this genre.

Perhaps no one anticipated how truly extraordinary the art quilt would become in such a short time. Seven Quilt Nationals before this one have hung at the Dairy Barn, and five have toured the world. Each one has inspired another tier of excellence, brought many new artists into the medium and served as a model for other juried quilt exhibitions. In little more than a decade, the art quilt has undergone a remarkable transformation to culminate in this eighth biennial Quilt National collection. So diverse, visionary and technically superb are the Quilt National '93 pieces that it is unquestionably the finest art-quilt show yet.

For a quilt to be considered for Quilt National '93, it must be original in design and concept. No matter how captivating, a straight rendition of the double wedding-ring pattern would not qualify. The

traditional quilt patterns and techniques may certainly influence a Quilt-National-caliber quilt. "There are all kinds of ways to push traditional design so it is new and fresh," says juror Judi Warren.

The 84 quilts chosen for this show go beyond those basic criteria to be superb examples of art. As the jurors' statement so aptly expresses it, a quilt chosen for this exhibition must offer an "innovative vocabulary of images" that "transform color and texture into dynamic patterns to provide new visual experiences" through "a learned and controlled responsiveness to the material."

"The first thing I look for in a Quilt National quilt is the visual aesthetic," says juror Elizabeth Busch. "I look at the design, composition and focus. Does it have substance? Is it powerful?" Next Busch looks at the craftsmanship, not only to see if it's technically good, but also to consider if it fits with the artist's vision. "Technically good doesn't mean the edges have to match," says Busch.

It would be presumptuous, even incorrect historically, to say that quilts such as the ones in Quilt National represent the first quilts that can be considered truly creative. That misconception stems from the fact that much of the tradition of quilting in the 20th century has encouraged a nostalgic copying of patterns developed by earlier quilt makers. But throughout history, the most honored quilt makers are those who brought new design and fresh perspective to the art.

Nor would it be correct to presume that the art quilts brought to light by Quilt Nationals are unique in their break from symmetrical patterning or traditional materials. The crazy quilts of the 1800s were anything but symmetrical or traditional for the time. And if they were displayed on a bed, it wasn't because the silk and embroidery-encrusted creations made practical bedspreads.

Without question, however, these contemporary quilts represent a turning point for both art and quilt making. Prior to 1971, when the Whitney Museum of American Art mounted a show of heritage quilt "art," quilt collections had never hung in fine-art museums nor had they been much addressed by art critics. Not until the first Quilt National had there ever been a juried exhibition of art quilts. Even then, although earlier Quilt Nationals certainly contained enduring works of art, as a whole the seminal collections weren't fully mature.

As you will see from the ensuing pages, Quilt National '93 is quilt art come of age. These works have the impact that can come only from the marriage of an artist's unique vision, technical mastery and sensitivity to design. "What we wanted to reward was the vitality of new expression and new risks," says juror Michael Monroe. "A few of the pieces may even outrage, but that's the way art moves forward, that's what keeps the dialogue lively," he adds. Forty-five percent of this year's artists are newcomers to Quilt National, which accounts in large part for the diversity among the pieces.

The Quilt National '93 collection is also a watershed exhibition from a technical perspective. "There has been a lot of evolution and experimentation in art quilts," says Busch, speaking of photo-transfer techniques, innovations in sewing machines, a seeming endless choices of fabrics, and new products for printing and dyeing cloth in the studio. "Artists are using a lot of processes and techniques but not just for the sake of process or technique. The ideas of the individual comes through in the materials."

As you look at this collection and read the artists' own words, you will experience the quilts on many different levels, from the impact of the imagery to richness of design to the power of the statement each work makes. But without question, you'll be treated to art as you may never have imagined it before. And if you have the good fortune to see the exhibition at the Dairy Barn or at one of its touring venues (see p. 88), you'll see first-hand that these unique works of art do indeed convey a special message.

—Sally Hayhow, Assistant to the Director of the Dairy Barn

Dorle Stern-Straeter
Munich, Germany
Bird's Paradise

Silk and cotton fabric,
some hand painted.
Machine pieced
and hand quilted.
63 in. by 65 in.

This quilt is part of a series of quilts based
on an original kite-shaped block, which I
tessellate by dividing it in half, first
horizontally and then vertically.

Jan Myers-Newbury
Pittsburgh, Pa.
Birch Eyes

Hand-dyed
cotton fabric.
Machine pieced and
machine quilted.
54 in. by 57 in.

Birch Eyes is a departure from the emphasis on color that has been a distinguishing feature of my quilts for 15 years. As I become more involved with tie-dyeing my fabrics, pattern has become more of a design consideration. The *shibori* panels in *Birch Eyes* are monumental and subtle at the same time, much the same as a forest of trees. The lack of color conveys a certain quietude that interests me.

AWARD FOR BEST OF SHOW

Ellen Oppenheimer
Oakland, Calif.
Neon Maze

Silk-screened and
hand-dyed fabric,
some over-dyed
commercial prints.
Machine pieced and
hand quilted.
48 in. by 50 in.

My "Neon Maze" series of quilts are textile
constructions in which a line or several lines
make a long and convoluted circuit or
journey through the quilt. Originally a
visual description of the complexity and
confusion that I perceive in my life, these
mazes have evolved into complex patterns
that are determined by fairly random rules
and parameters.

**DOMINI McCARTHY
MEMORIAL AWARD**

Arturo Alonzo Sandoval
Lexington, Ky.
Lady Liberty/Babylon II

Cibachrome photographs, webbing, acetate transparencies, netting, threads, paint, fabric and adhesive. Machine pieced and stitched. 60 in. by 86 in.

My political imagery addresses issues of nuclear war, terrorism and government corruption. Using drawing and collage to create my imagery allows me to develop a contemporary artistic statement with high-tech photo-imaging materials. Working in this manner creates color, texture and form not possible with more traditional materials. My quilts are meant to be both beautiful and informative.

MOST INNOVATIVE USE OF THE MEDIUM AWARD
Sponsored by Friends of Fiber Art International

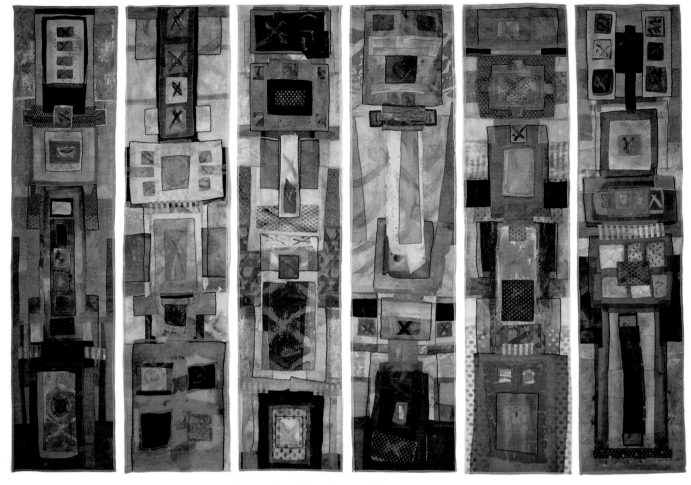

Emily Richardson
Philadelphia, Pa.
Then We Were Six

Silk organza, raw
silk, cotton, other
fibers, cotton yarn and
twine, embroidery
floss, thread, acrylic
paint and chalk.
Painted and stained,
appliquéd, couched
and embroidered
by hand.
107 in. by 73 in.

Each panel in this quilt, although standing
as a complete unit, functions as a vital
part of the whole. The piece reflects the way
in which members of a family exhibit
similar qualities of appearance and nature
while distinguishing themselves as
individuals. *Then We Were Six* is rooted in
my own family experience.

Alison Schwabe
Englewood, Colo.
Ora Banda

Cotton and blended
fabric, some spray
painted, others hand
dyed by Deborah
Lunn. Machine
pieced and hand
quilted.
62 in. by 50 in.

Our family once lived in Ora Banda in
western Australia, a semi-desert region of
red-browns, tans and creamy pinks with
vegetation of small eucalyptus and grey-
green saltbush. Every few years, after heavy
rains, the desert blooms with brightly
colored flowers. This quilt is a memory
of the many years we spent in that
harsh beauty.

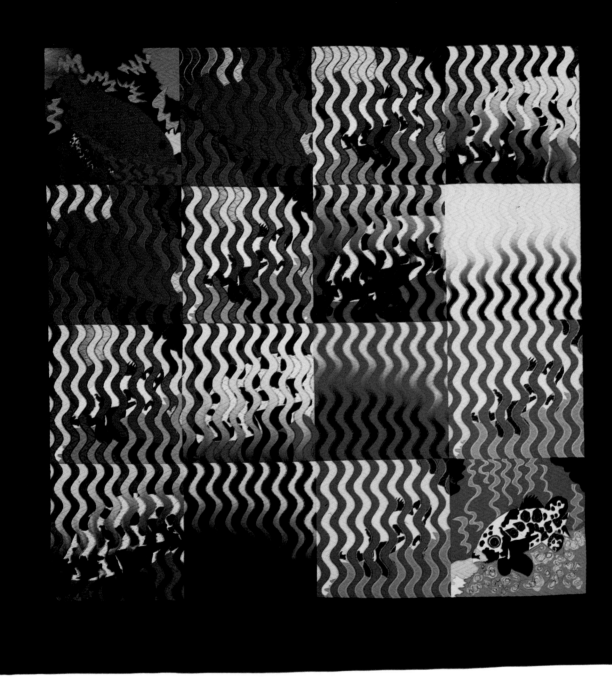

Pauline Burbidge
Nottingham,
England
Sink or Swim

Cotton fabrics, some
hand dyed. Pieced,
appliquéd and
quilted by machine.
78 in. by 77 in.

This work was part of a series of quilts that I
made on the theme of fish, water and
movement. I began by making paper
collages of two fish—Coral Trout and
Clown Sweetlips. These were my starting
images, and I began to intercut them to
create a water-like effect.

Nancy Crasco
Arlington, Mass.
Black Mayonnaise

Cotton fabric over-
dyed with Procion
dyes, transparent
synthetic overlays.
Hand and machine
pieced, hand
appliquéd and
hand quilted.
72 in. by 38 in.

This is the fourth piece in a series of
quilts about the state of the earth. *Black
Mayonnaise,* a term used by divers, refers to
the substance that can be dredged from the
bottom of our harbors and bays.

**Magdalena
Krajewska**
Warsaw, Poland
Yellow into Black

Hand-dyed natural
and synthetic fabrics.
Machine pieced and
appliquéd.
58 in. by 80 in.

Color and image come from looking
at things against the sun, with your
eyes closed.

Patty Hawkins
Lyons, Colo.
*Indian Gap Near
Lyons II*

Cotton, blended and
lamé fabrics, thread
and glass beads.
Machine pieced
using inlaid
construction,
machine quilted.
77 in. by 55 in.

The beauty of our Colorado mountains
made me realize that what's under our very
noses is often overlooked. With the repeated
drive to rural Lyons, I was challenged to
create the local mountain beauty through
spatial images and visual texture. Inlaid
construction allows for more freedom in
design and is related to putting jigsaw
puzzle pieces together.

Linda R. MacDonald
Willits, Calif.
Spotted Owl vs. Chain Saw — Wild & Tasty

Cotton fabric, dyed, airbrushed and painted. Hand and machine quilted. 51 in. by 65 in.

Spotted Owl vs. Chain Saw is one of three quilts dealing with conflicts occurring now in the Northwest. The use of a can and the image of a cooked spotted owl take the piece into the realm of a political cartoon. Loggers, intent on logging first and being concerned with the environment second, might applaud this piece, while environmentalists can appreciate the grim future for the owl if excessive logging continues.

M. Joan Lintault
Carbondale, Ill.
In the Grass

Hand-dyed, screen-
printed and painted
cotton fabric. Machine
pieced and quilted,
hand embellished
with beads.
91 in. by 98 in.

I begin with white fabric because I see its
possibilities. I dye, print and paint my own
images and feel free to use any technique
that contributes to my work. I do not reject a
technique simply because it is laborious. I
base my work on geological rather than TV
time. Here I have chosen flowers and insects
to bring perpetual summer indoors: the cool
of the forest, the heat in the meadow, the
whine of the insects, and the nasty things
waiting in the grass.

Mary Mashuta
Berkeley, Calif.
*Exploration: Learning
to Get Along*

Striped fabric
purchased in
Durban, South
Africa. Machine
pieced and machine
quilted with
monofilament and
Sulky rayon thread.
72 in. by 70 in.

I am presently exploring optical designs that
can be created with stripes. Getting to know
the stripes I was working with was like
getting to know people with whom I am
unfamiliar. Whether the stripes were
difficult or easy to work with, fancy or plain
to look at, all of them contributed to the
appearance of the finished quilt. This work
was made in response to the riots in south
central Los Angeles following the Rodney
King verdict.

Judy Becker
Newton, Mass.
Only in New York

Italian cotton chintz.
Machine pieced and
hand quilted.
59 in. by 46 in.

Only in New York do I feel like a total
tourist, racing to store up the visual
overload of its museums, galleries, street
people and store fronts. Back in my studio, I
try to resolve the whirl of impressions from
my yearly trip. Only in New York do I find
such exciting material to start this new quilt.

Marilyn L. Harrison
Boca Raton, Fla.
Bolts of Cloth

Viscose rayon twill satin, Procion dye and Cloud Cover fabric paint with paste resist. Machine and hand quilted. 74 in. by 43 in.

The title *Bolts of Cloth* flashed into my mind while I was sketching another work. Such inspiration is a gift, and I needed only a trip to the hardware store to find enough types of bolts, nuts and washers to balance the composition. The design recalls ceremonial icons and gives the bolts a surreal presence.

Ann Brauer
Charlemont, Mass.
*If I Should Fall in Love
With You*

Silk and wool fabrics.
Machine sewn one
piece at a time to
muslin backing.
38 in. by 44 in.

Everyone has memories of quilts. In my
work I am trying to use the intensity and
humanness of these memories to create
meanings that go beyond the actual design.
In this piece I was exploring the relationship
of the two turquoise shapes that almost fit
together. They are surrounded by dancing
dreams or spirits, which are based on the
traditional log-cabin pattern.

Maryanne Ellison Simmons
Chesterfield, Mo.
American Landscapes: Mapping Series/ 40-Acre Plots

Fabric is printed using lithographic plates, collagraph and monoprint techniques. Beads are sewn at intersecting pencil lines with simple tacking. 30 in. by 41 in.

This work is about the displacement of peoples and the documents that presage it. It is about the organization of an unwieldy territory into base lines and meridians, square-mile sectors and the remnants that remain of those sectors. My studio sits on one of these—a 40-acre plot owned since the late 19th century by a succession of widows.

Marianne Lehmann-Hörler

Affoltern am Albis, Switzerland
Najanda

Hand-dyed cotton and hand-painted silk fabrics. Machine pieced, hand quilted and hand embroidered. 52 in. by 48 in.

In this quilt I have tried to express the sensuousness of the fabrics. Delicate differences in the structure of the fabrics and their absorption of light generate subtle feelings. It is a composition in which the changing intensity of tones and colors, the concentration of light and dark values as well as the contrast of calm and animated elements allow the viewer the freedom to reflect on the work.

Joyce Marquess Carey

Madison, Wis.
Passing Through

Satin, silk, polyester
and rayon fabrics.
Machine pieced.
54 in. by 45 in.

Passing Through is
one in a series called
"Crossroads." This work
represents pathways, choices, obstacles and
unexpected turns in the road. There is no
clear-cut way to move from one path to
another and no definite "starting place,"
although the paths can easily be traced to
their origins, one's past history.

Barbara Lydecker Crane
Lexington, Mass.
Conversion

A combination of hand-dyed, hand-painted and commercial cotton fabrics. Machine pieced, hand appliquéd, machine and hand quilted. 47 in. by 67 in.

Depicting a transformation of missiles to houses against a changing sky, this quilt represents my hope for economic conversion in this time of reduced military threat and rising human needs.

Constance Scheele
Katy, Tex.
Metamorphosis

Commercial and
hand-dyed cottons
and silk fabrics.
Machine pieced and
machine quilted.
Fabrics dyed by
Eric Morti and
Constance Scheele.
61 in. by 44 in.

This quilt was done using a color palette
taken from triple-dyed silk noil fabrics. They
were dyed using rust, gold and black dyes
but, because of the nature of the process,
produced a wide range of colors with which
to work.

**Deborah Melton
Anderson**

Columbus, Ohio
The Back Boathouse

Images photographed
by the artist and
transferred onto
cotton fabric. Hand
and machine
appliquéd and
machine quilted.
42 in. by 54 in.

I have used photo-transfer images to
document a variety of views of the family's
boathouse, built early in this century in
McGregor Bay on Lake Huron. After
seasonal ice eroded the concrete pillars
supporting the log and board structure, log
cribs filled with rocks were added to the
pillars. It was the patterns of the cribs that
drew me to discover the structural beauty of
the back boathouse.

Barbara Bushey
Ypsilanti, Mich.
*Scraps of Time: Dome
of the Rock III*

Hand-dyed polyester,
linen, cotton and
ribbon. Machine
and hand stitched,
burned and melted.
9 in. by 6 in.

During the summer of 1990, I taught my
way from England to Egypt as part of
Eastern Michigan University's Cultural
History Tour. Seeing so many great works of
art on three continents was an incredible
experience, sometimes nearly overwhelming.

This piece is part of an on-going series of
impressions of my journey. *Scraps of Time*
comes from brief encounters with a variety
of objects that have existed for a long time,
as well as from my method of working.

Ardyth Davis
Leesburg, Va.
Horizon X/Amber

Painted, pleated,
stitched silk, piping
cord and filling.
Hand and machine
stitched, hand
quilted.
48 in. by 32 in.

This piece reflects my ongoing interest in
painting and texturing cloth. Using
landscape as reference enables me to explore
not only color but also various ways to
structure the ridged surface that has become

an important aspect of my work. I have also
been intrigued by the idea of revealing
something of the nature of the quilt's inner
layer, hence the stitching around the piled
piping cord under the pleated surface.

Deborah J. Felix
Berkeley, Calif.
Object of Love

Fabric, paint and
pastels. Reverse
appliquéd and
stitched by hand.
48 in. by 96 in.

For over a year I worked on a series of
pieces that depict all the objects that I have
around me and that I have come to love.

Each object has a personality and plays an
important part of my life.

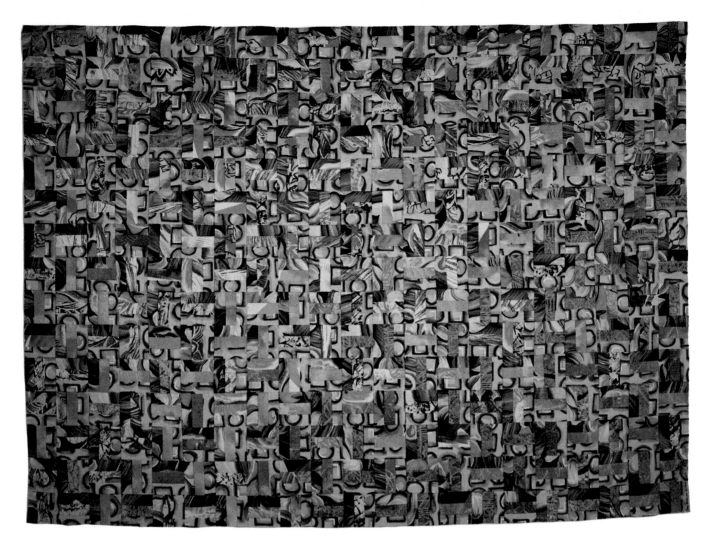

Meiny Vermaas-Van der Heide

Tempe, Ariz.
Southwest V: A Green Quilt

Cotton fabrics. Machine pieced and machine quilted. 82 in. by 59 in.

To me, a quilt series is a challenge—a step-by-step exploration of possibilities within a limited set of options. Pieces in the "Southwest" series combine dark scribbles on a pale background with elements gathered from my study of double positive/negative images in quilt making. The Green Quilt label stands for environmental concern brought about in a positive, open-ended way.

Therese May
San Jose, Calif.
Playful Contemplation

Assorted fabrics,
acrylic paint, fabric
paint, buttons, beads
and other
embellishments.
Machine appliquéd,
hand embellished.
86 in. by 56 in.

Looking back, looking forward
To the past, to the future
Being reborn into the present
Growing, being contained
Playful contemplation
Loving every minute

Terrie Hancock Mangat
Cincinnati, Ohio
Helen Stice Memorial

Various fabrics, embellishments and found objects. Reverse appliquéd, embroidered. Quilted by Sue Rule. Chest built by Scott Humphrey.
66 in. by 94 in. by 16 in.

I met Helen Stice when she was 93 years old. She was making her funeral dress. When a museum wanted to show her eclectic work, she had a new zest for life. She is one of my inspirations in that she expresses her vision with whatever material strikes her fancy. She selected ingredients for their color, texture and power of association.

Judith H. Perry
Winnetka, Ill.
True Poems Flee

Hand-dyed and
commercial cotton
and synthetic fabrics.
Machine pieced,
machine quilted and
hand lettered.
47 in. by 43 in.

"To see the summer sky is poetry
Though never in a book it lie
True poems flee."
— *Emily Dickinson*

This is what the artist strives for: to capture
the uncapturable, to grasp that which is out
of our reach, to comprehend the
incomprehensible. I am always trying to
capture the poetry.

Libby Lehman
Houston, Tex.
Impact!

Commercial and
hand-dyed cottons,
rayon and metallic
threads (tons of
both!). Machine
pieced, machine
appliquéd and
machine quilted.
71 in. by 81 in.

Impact! depicts the sudden collision of our
ordered lives with forces unexpected and
beyond our control. We cannot prevent this
impact, but we can choose to turn it into a
positive force for the future.

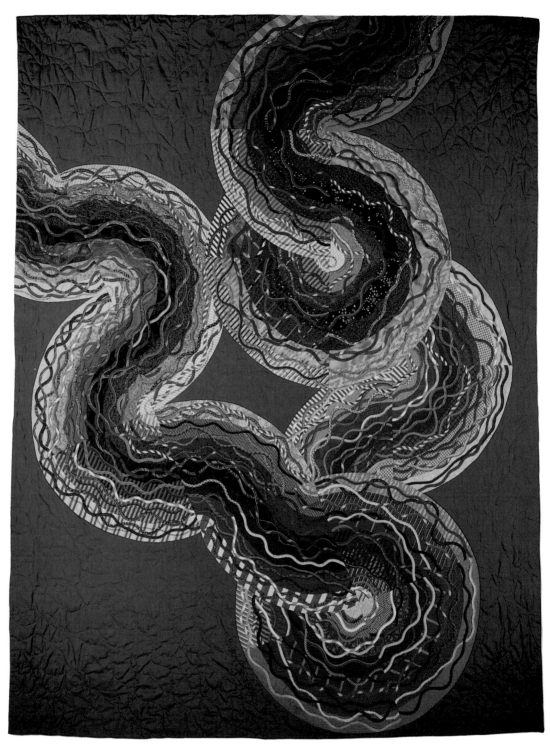

Marion Ongerth
Berkeley, Calif.
South Central L.A.

Cotton and blended
fabrics. Machine
pieced, machine
quilted and machine
appliquéd. Machine
quilted by Rebecca
Rohrkaste.
64 in. by 85 in.

South Central L.A. can be seen as both a giant
fireball and a map of the various areas of
Los Angeles that erupted in violence and
burning in response to the verdict in the trial
of the policemen who beat Rodney King.

I chose colors that would depict the hottest
places in a flame as well as the smoky areas,
and let the surface design create the frantic
energy and tension.

Judy Hooworth
Sydney, Australia
Composition in Yellow

Cotton fabrics.
Machine pieced,
hand and machine
quilted.
81 in. by 83 in.

The juxtaposition of color and pattern has always intrigued me, particularly bold color and strongly patterned fabrics. Yellow is my favorite color, and I use it all the time in my quilts. For me it is the color of life and energy.

Steve Hohenboken
Bloomington, Ind.
Preoccupation

Fabric and clothing.
Machine pieced,
appliquéd and
machine quilted.
59 in. by 74 in.

In my work I often explore the idea of giving and receiving comfort—physical, spiritual and emotional—and the ways and places we try to find comfort for ourselves.

As I worked on this piece, I remembered my adolescence and the restless hours I spent at night trying to reconcile confusing feelings and beliefs.

Elaine Plogman
Cincinnati, Ohio
Incendiary City

Cotton and blended
fabrics. Machine
pieced, appliquéd,
embroidered and
quilted.
45 in. by 54 in.

While working on this quilt, I was becoming
increasingly discouraged with the moral
decline I was seeing around me and with
the corresponding breakdown of traditional
institutions. The Los Angeles riots, both in
cause and effect, were the final blow that led
me to add the appliquéd flames to the
central columnar shape.

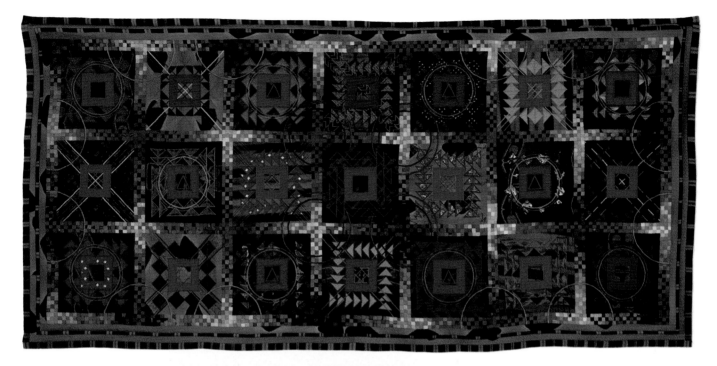

Rosemary P. Bathurst

Eaton Rapids, Mich.
Cubed Geese IV

Cotton fabrics.
Machine pieced,
appliquéd,
embroidered and
machine quilted.
85 in. by 40 in.

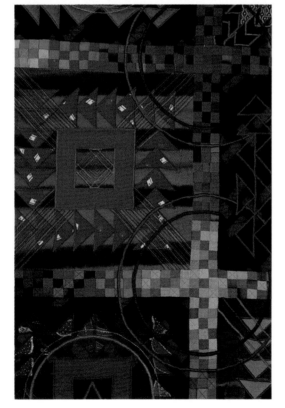

This quilt continues work with familiar symbols. The open, red square in the center of each block is a new character, inspired by traditional sources whose use of the red square represents the hearth/fire in our own dwellings/life. The surface layering is a formal response to challenges, such as using historically influenced cloth from other cultures and embellishing it by machine stitchery, a technology of my culture.

Nancy Herman
Merion, Pa.
Tipsy

Assorted fabrics.
Strip-pieced, layered,
machine quilted
and cut.
48 in. by 91 in.

In this work, light is moving from top to
bottom inside the boxes. I wanted to give
the feeling that light was spilling from one
to the other and contained by texture on the
outside. To accentuate the "tipsy" feeling, I
tried to use colors and prints that are a little
disturbing.

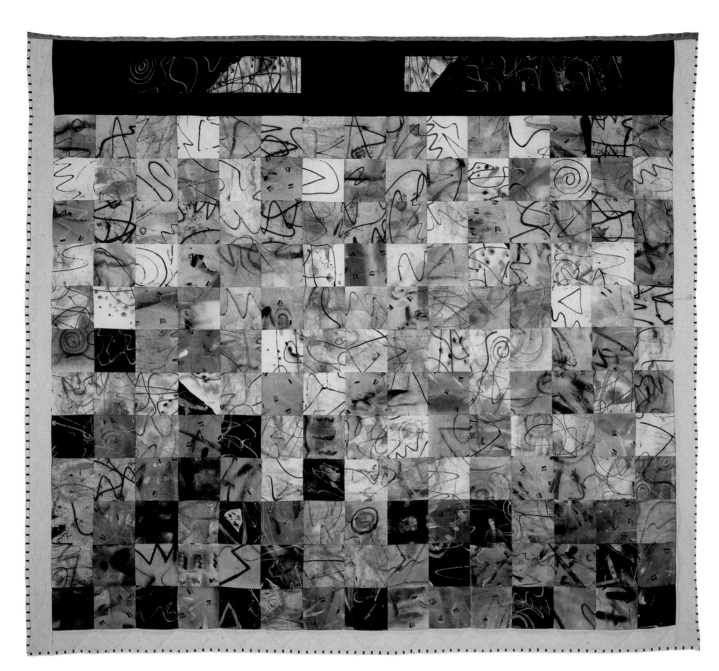

Mary Allen Chaisson

South Harpswell, Maine

White Rock
Commercial and hand-painted cotton and blended fabrics with some copy-machine transfers and monoprinting. Machine pieced, hand quilted, appliquéd and tied. 52 in. by 46 in.

This piece is a reaction to many hikes in and around New Mexico's Pajarito Plateau, where the juxtaposition of our nuclear age and prehistoric Indian times is ever present. I like to take fragments from the past and present them in a contemporary manner.

Sally A. Sellers
Vancouver, Wash.
HomeBody

Commercial cotton
and synthetic fabrics.
Machine appliquéd
on canvas.
59 in. by 56 in.

This image arose at a time when I was
forced to confront a number of issues
including, most painfully, our inability to
always protect our children. My seven-year-
old daughter, Kate, had medical problems so
severe that I could no longer care for her in
our home. Her move to the hospital violated
my maternal instinct at the deepest level.
The small milagro in the "doorway" of the
house/woman is the image of a little girl.

**Susan Shie
and James Acord**
Wooster, Ohio
*The Year of the
Monkey and the
Camel; a Green Quilt*

Hand-painted and
commercial fabrics,
glass beads, natural
gemstones, poly clay,
hand-tooled and
dyed leather.
Pieced, quilted and
embroidered by both
hand and machine.
55 in. by 62 in. (From
a private collection;
courtesy Mobilia
Gallery.)

This quilt began on the Monkey Chinese
New Year and is an Earth Healer's Primer. It
honors all the wise animals, our best
teachers in respecting our Earth Home.
Trusting each other is the first step. The
central monkey figures hold the future and
they "see" out of their hearts—with second
faces where their chests would be.

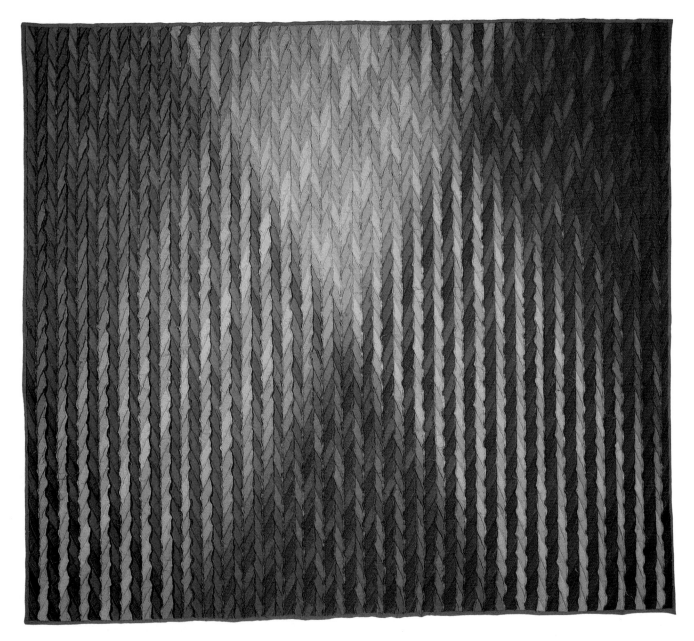

Inge Hueber
Cologne, Germany
Rainbow Rhythm I

Hand-dyed cotton.
Machine pieced and
hand quilted.
73 in. by 63 in.

Colors are the motivation of my work. For me they are not attributes or illustrations, but are themselves alive and create a variety of interactions. Colored fabrics attract me in a very direct way. I want to express their special characteristics and possibilities. I regard my quilts as an expression of my joy of living.

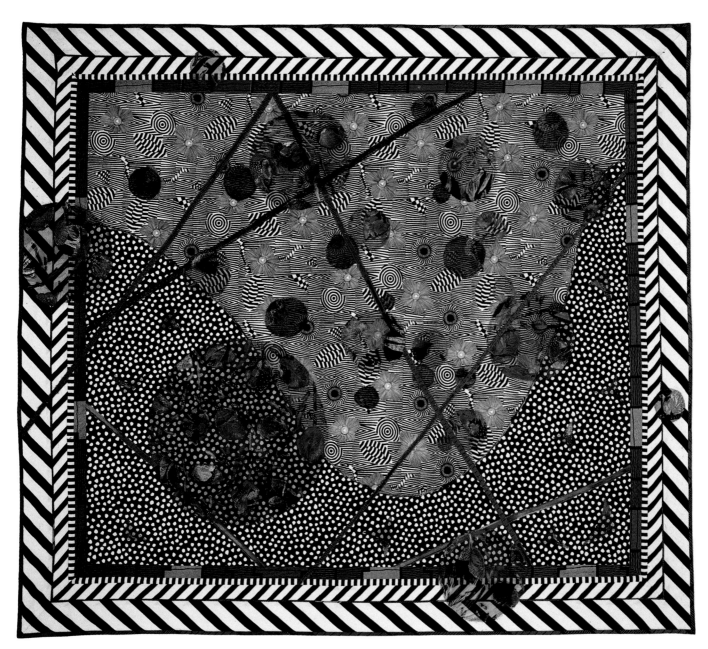

Judy Zoelzer Levine
Bayside, Wis.
Coming Into Being

Cotton, silk and
synthetic fabrics and
yarns. Pieced,
appliquéd and
quilted by machine.
52 in. by 46 in.

This work developed intuitively. As I
worked with the fabric, I realized that my
selections represented my thoughts at the
moment. Some thoughts were fleeting,
others were more substantive. Some are
mere fragments that never made it to
consciousness.

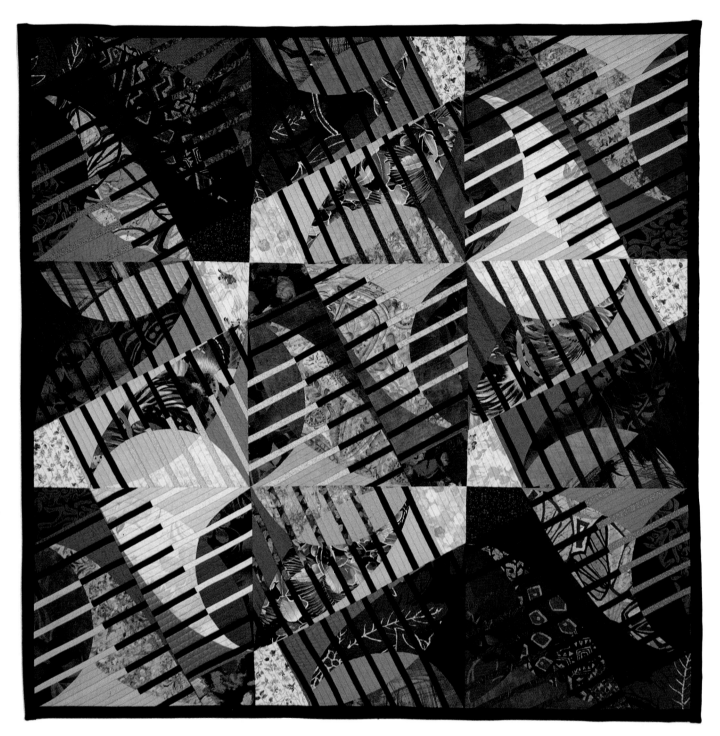

Trudy L. Bergen
Los Angeles, Calif.
Elegy for Thelma

Commercial cotton
and blended fabrics,
some hand-dyed by
Eric Morti. Machine
pieced and machine
quilted.
54 in. by 53 in.

Elegy for Thelma commemorates the life of
my mother, Thelma Mae Bishop Bergen
(1920-1978). It grew out of my recent work
on the theme of suburban culture. While
most of these recent quilts have dealt with
the social realm and the dominance of
popular culture, this quilt explores the very
personal issue of how a woman chooses to
construct her life within the social
framework of her time.

Karen Larsen
Cambridge, Mass.
Wool Crazy 8 —Three Part Harmony

Wool with cotton
back and synthetic
batting. Hand and
machine pieced and
machine quilted;
embellished with
pleating, weaving
and buttons.
108 in. by 75 in.

This quilt is meant to pay homage to the
folk singing of Gordon Bok, Ann Mayo Muir
and Ed Trickett, who periodically tour
together as a trio. The patterns and color
placement mimic the ways in which
harmony works; sometimes one voice is
dominant, sometimes all are of equal
intensity. Specific shapes and fabrics were
inspired by the rich tones and textures of
their voices.

Joan Schulze
Sunnyvale, Calif.
Great Women

Cotton, silk, netting, lint and miscellaneous fabrics. Photo-transfer images; hand and machine stitched. 30 in. by 38 in.

Men, the history books lead us to believe, created the great works of art, made the most important discoveries, formed civilizations and ruled the world. I wanted to celebrate all those women who quietly did great things while bearing children and providing inspiration for others.

Dominie Nash
Bethesda, Md.
Two Solitudes

Cotton, silk and
rayon fabrics treated
with dyes, inko-
printing and screen
printing. Machine
appliquéd and
machine quilted.
57 in. by 56 in.

The title of this work refers to the poet
Rilke's definition of love: "Love consists in
this: that two solitudes protect and touch
and greet each other." I came across this
quote while working on this piece. As far as
I knew, the design was abstract. However,
when it was finished, two figures appeared.

Rhoda R. Cohen
Weston, Mass.
Unrestricted Particles

Hand-dyed and
commercial cotton
and blended fabrics.
Hand appliquéd and
hand quilted.
60 in. by 76 in.

This design is intended to expand the idea
of the relationship of fabrics, the way
irregular shapes interact. It is arranged to
have the look of clustered shards of fabric
that are not tightly controlled from outside
but seem to have a plasticity, an inner
compulsion, holding them in a fluid
suspension.

**Barbara Oliver
Hartman**
Flower Mound, Tex.
Fallscape

Cotton fabric.
Machine appliquéd
and machine quilted.
40 in. by 30 in.

Jane A. Sassaman
Chicago, Ill.
Heaven and Earth

Cotton and blended
fabrics. Machine
pieced and machine
quilted.
64 in. by 64 in.

This quilt examines the relationship between heaven and earth. Heaven is depicted in religious paintings by golden radiating lines. So in this quilt, too, heaven is a traditional idealized representation—all powerful and perfect. It radiates over the green planet, which seems to be self-sufficient and oblivious to the invisible and immeasurable influence of the spirit.

This piece is part of a series of landscapes. *Fallscape* utilizes raw edges, layers and thread to create the look of texture in the landscape.

Erika Carter
Bellevue, Wash.
Nurturing

Cotton fabrics.
Machine pieced,
hand and machine
appliquéd and
machine quilted.
51 in. by 51 in.

Mankind tends to place itself at the top of
the natural ladder. Putting hands on the
ends of my tree branches implies my need to
re-evaluate this sequence. These hands also
suggest my identification with tree imagery.
Trees nurture our environment, and I, a
mother, nurture my family.

Robin Schwalb
Brooklyn, N.Y.
The Gift of Tongues

Commercial cottons and silk, photo silkscreened, marbleized and stenciled. Machine pieced, hand appliquéd by artist, hand quilted by Grace Miller. 54 in. by 98 in. Photograph used in quilt: *Controlled Demolition*; Bruce Chatwin, *The Songlines* (Viking Penguin, 1987).

I'm not sure which came first: the photograph of a dynamited, collapsing skyscraper, or a quote from Bruce Chatwin's *The Songlines*, "…language…the gift of tongues…has a rebellious and wayward vitality compared to which the foundations of the Pyramid are as dust," but they cried out to be used together. But what does it mean? Is it nothing more than a self-portrait of a blabbermouth? You decide.

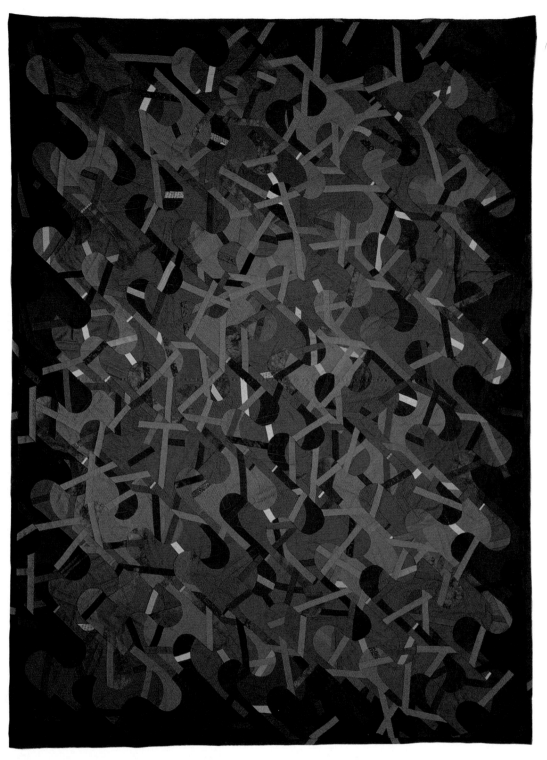

Fiona Gavens
Whiteman Creek,
Australia
*Bush Fragments III:
After the Rain*

Hand-dyed cotton and blended fabrics. Machine pieced and machine quilted. 39 in. by 53 in.

Having lived on 50 acres "in the bush" for more than 14 years, I feel I have absorbed the colors and feel of our place almost by osmosis. I love the complex mixture of broad impression and tiny details, seemingly at random and yet with an underlying structure and order. The paddocks look empty from a distance, but the closer you get, the more detail is revealed.

Carol Drummond
Sarasota, Fla.
Guardian

Cotton and blended
fabrics, paint and
buttons. Machine
pieced, machine
appliquéd, hand
appliquéd and
hand quilted.
32 in. by 29 in.

Most of my work is done spontaneously,
and its meaning is revealed to me as it
draws toward completion. Guardian Angels
are always good to call upon when needed.
I prefer my images to be somewhat vague
so that viewers can draw their own
interpretations. This quilt was conceived
while waiting to see the course Hurricane
Andrew would take as it approached the
Florida coastline.

Anne Triguba
Lancaster, Ohio
Hiding Places II

Cotton and blended
fabrics. Machine
pieced and hand
appliquéd; hand
quilted by Liz Foster.
60 in. by 60 in.

This quilt was my first attempt at machine
piecing, and it opened doors to new
techniques and skills. Also, I found an
overwhelming excitement in using small
fabric areas to create new design elements.
I developed a strong emotional connection
to the piece, which was another new
experience for me. It gave me the energy to
work nonstop until it was finished, and an
intense sense of happiness and peace upon
its completion.

Lynne Sward
Virginia Beach, Va.
*There's No Place
Like…*

Cotton and blended
fabrics, fusible web.
Machine and hand
appliquéd, machine
quilted.
41 in. by 38 in.

It all started with dreaming of houses on
water…magic…meditations…metaphysicas
…subconscious…past lives…Egypt…Native
America…life force…snow-capped
mountain retreats…words spoken and
unspoken…love of life…universal
brotherhood…infinite cosmos…. There's no
place like….

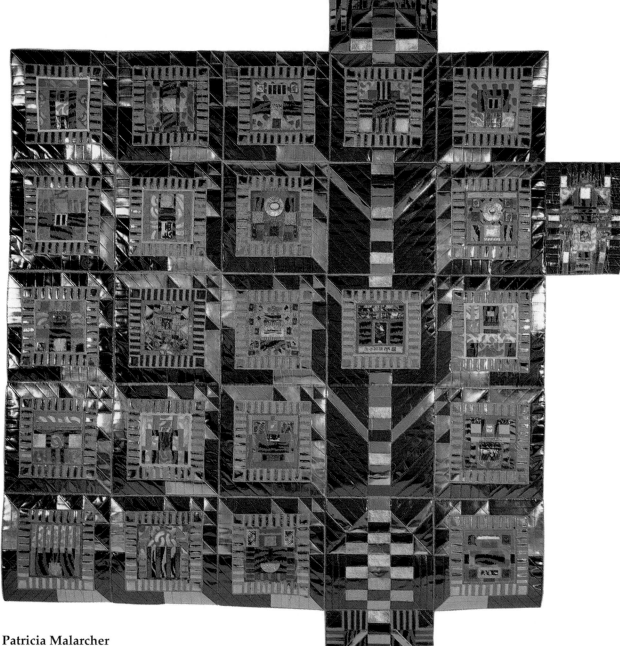

Patricia Malarcher
Englewood, N.J.
*Rapunzel Sings the
Tiger Rag*

Mylar, linen, painted
canvas, gold leaf,
transfer prints,
ready-made fabric
elements. Machine
and hand sewn.
70 in. by 78 in.

Ambiguous references, some
alluding to the Grimm brothers' tale of
Rapunzel, are open to interpretation.

Sue Alvarez
Charlotte, N.C.
Pleasure Seekers

Commercial cotton
fabrics and glass
beads. Machine
pieced, machine
quilted and hand
embellished.
59 in. by 67 in.

Pleasure Seekers is an exercise in quilt making
through the eyes of band students with
their constant movement and endless
formations. The beadwork on this quilt
draws you to its spiritual center. We are
reminded of the need we all have to touch
and seek pleasure.

Risë Nagin
Pittsburgh, Pa.
Three Sisters

Silk, polyester,
cotton, rayon and
textile and acrylic
paints. Layered,
appliquéd, quilted
and embroidered by
hand.
94 in. by 72 in.

My intention is to create beautiful and
complex surfaces that evoke some aspect of
human experience. Perhaps it is something
as simple as the quality of light in a foggy
landscape or, as in recent work, the use of
symbolic narrative suggesting the nature of
inner realities.

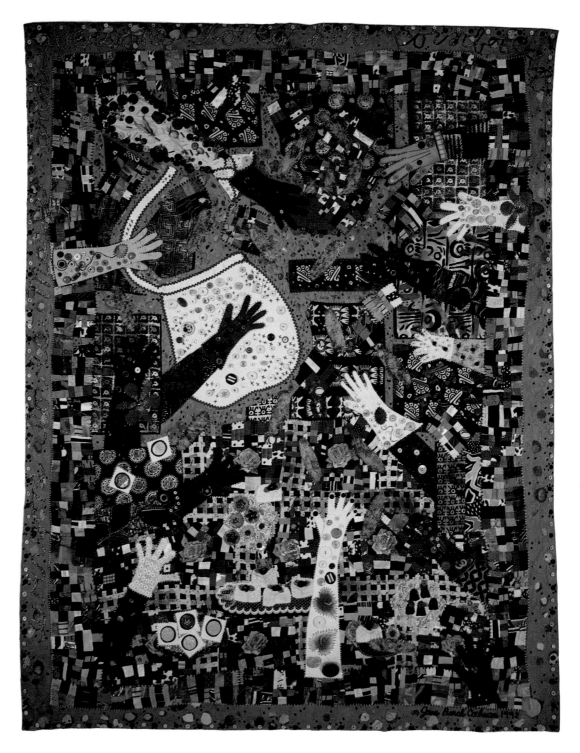

Jane Burch Cochran
Rabbit Hash, Ky.
Southern Devotion

Various fabrics,
beads, buttons,
paint, clothing and
found objects.
Machine pieced,
hand appliquéd,
hand embellished
and hand quilted.
68 in. by 85 in.

Southern Devotion is my third quilt in a series
called "Food for Thought." This quilt pays
homage to one of my favorite people, Marie
Sims, of Clover, Virginia. Just as the hands
(gloves) reach past the fancy party food
for her cornbread sticks, many in her
community reach to Marie for both physical
and spiritual nurturing.

Sandra Townsend Donabed
Wellesley Hills, Mass.
Zebra Mussels

Cotton fabrics
and thread
embellishments.
Hand and machine
pieced, hand
appliquéd and
machine quilted.
54 in. by 39 in.

Carried over the Atlantic in ships' ballast
water, the zebra mussel has invaded all the
Great Lakes in just a few short years. They
are clogging sewage-water outlets and fresh-
water intakes, purification systems and even
ship engines. So far there is no method of
control that doesn't harm the indigenous
species. My quilt depicts an underwater area
of the now relatively unpolluted Lake Erie
where zebra mussels are thriving.

Elizabeth A. Busch
Bangor, Maine
Tide Pool

Canvas treated with
textile ink and
colored pastels.
Machine pieced
and quilted.
63 in. by 34 in.
(From the collection
of Peter Brooks.)

Karen N. Soma
Seattle, Wash.
Light and Leaf

Cotton fabrics, hand-
dyed and screen-
printed with
additional dyes.
Machine pieced and
machine quilted.
58 in. by 41 in.

Since childhood, I have been fascinated with the way light and shadow transform color and set up patterns and rhythms that shift and change with the time of day, passing clouds, or a freshening breeze. With this piece, I think of a hot summer's afternoon, a long row of raspberry bushes, the sharp smell and taste of the fruit, the dazzle of sun on the tops of the hedge, the cool shadows below.

Tiny worlds of exotic color, curious shapes and alien creatures form in the giant granite cups that stay filled with salt water and life as the sea recedes on the coast of Maine. *Tide Pool* is my view into one of these quiet, mysterious realms.

INVITATIONAL: Quilt National '93 Juror

Fran Skiles
Plantation, Fla.
Passing Through

Cotton duck fabric,
fabric and acrylic
paint, resist and silk,
photo transfers,
Polaroid negative
transfer. Machine
appliquéd and
machine quilted.
45 in. by 50 in.

Passing Through is a construction that reflects
impressions of nature and the home. What
began as a passive and orderly design
ended in my reaction to the destruction of
Hurricane Andrew.

Adrien Rothschild
Baltimore, Md.
Purple Mountains

Hand-dyed cotton
fabrics. Machine
pieced and hand
quilted.
71 in. by 88 in.

The two major influences on my work are
the paintings of my mother, Amalie
Rothschild, and the tessellated designs of
M.C. Escher. Perhaps my eye for light and
color derives from my neurophysiology. I
suffer from Seasonal Affective Disorder,

becoming depressed and lethargic in the
absence of light. Light makes me happy, and
I delight in color play when designing
my quilts.

Jane Dunnewold
San Antonio, Tex.
The Fortitude of Motherhood

Photocopied images transferred to silk broadcloth. Silk-screened, machine quilted and embellished with straight pins and burned edges.
43 in. by 50 in.

I have recently been working with issues related to motherhood and "femaleness" in this culture. Through my work, I hope to unravel mixed messages thrust upon us by the culture, while studying the ambivalent feelings we, as women, have about roles both chosen and assumed.

Judi Warren
Maumee, Ohio
The Mountain and the Magic: A Color Not Forgotten

Cotton, silk, lamé, antique kimono silk, ribbons and beads. Machine pieced and hand quilted. 69 in. by 86 in.

This work is part of a continuing series called "The Mountain and The Magic." *A Color Not Forgotten* uses overlapping geometric elements and landscape imagery—sky, clouds, mountains, sea and leaves, both vibrant and fading, expressing change and memory. The mountain is Fuji-san; the magic is Japan.

INVITATIONAL: Quilt National '93 juror

Lenore Davis
Newport, Ky.
Diamond and Cross

Cotton velveteen,
metallic thread,
textile paint and dye.
Monotyped, painted
and hand quilted
with tailor's collar
stitch.
56 in. by 56 in.

Diamond and Cross, a whole-cloth quilt,
reflects patchwork in that the center square
is a collection of patterns, printed one at a
time, as if they were pieced. The gathered
cloth impressions on the frame area are
achieved by a rubbing technique. The red

color, symmetrical organization and the idea
of small units and symbols are inspired by
the rich and complex surfaces of Oriental
carpets. The metallic threads glaze the
surface with an allover stitch that marries
with the design and materials.

Sharon Heidingsfelder
Little Rock, Ark.
Allegheny Moon

Commercial and silk-screened cotton fabric. Machine pieced and machine quilted. 78 in. by 78 in.

This quilt represents a milestone in my quilting life. It is the first quilt I have made since I tore down and rebuilt my studio two years ago. This quilt is also the first quilt that I have quilted myself, albeit by machine. What freedom to be able to change lines of quilting when the design is not as good as I imagined.

Charlotte Patera
Grass Valley, Calif.
Hocus Pocus

Commercial and
hand-dyed cotton
fabrics. Machine
pieced and hand
quilted.
44 in. by 51 in.

My work is inspired by my strong interest in
the *mola* art done by the Kuna Indian
women of San Blas, Panama. I like to
reinvent the *mola*, finding new ways of
using it in my quilt art.

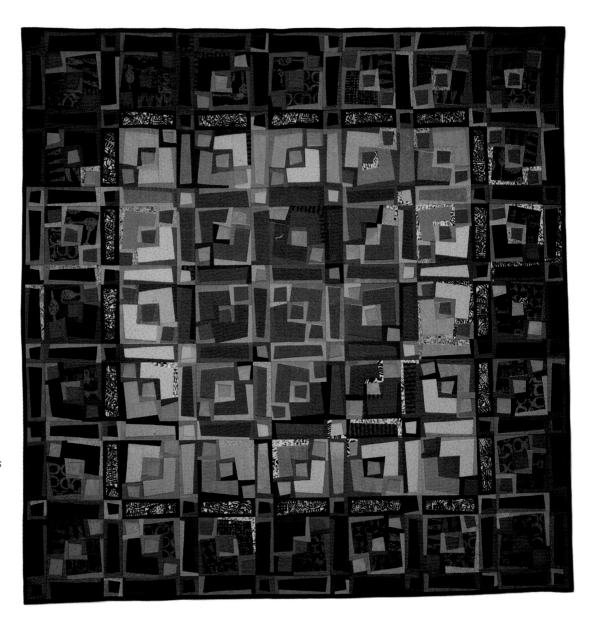

Liz Axford
Houston, Tex.
Freehand 4: Luminous Numinous

Commercial and hand-dyed cotton fabrics. Machine pieced, machine quilted and hand embellished with linen thread and African wax block prints.
70 in. by 70 in.
(From the collection of Gail and Lloyd Evans.)

My "Freehand" series is an attempt to capture simple, geometric, vaguely architectural doodles in fabric. *Freehand 4: Luminous Numinous* began with an original variation of the traditional log-cabin block.

I improvised as I constructed each block. The machine quilting, loosely based on the irregular patterns of Shoowa embroidered textiles from Zaire, was designed at the sewing machine.

Cindy Carroll
Park Ridge, Ill.
Rainforest I

Cotton fabric,
threads and glass
beads. Machine
pieced, machine
quilted and hand
embellished.
61 in. by 51 in.

I cut and assemble my quilts with relatively little planning, trusting that my own instincts about the fabrics I have chosen will be good. The blocks I design and the overall colors of my subjects are the only structure I impose on my work. What happens when I let a piece develop without a lot of personal interference is always interesting and far better than anything I could have planned.

Merrill Mason
Jersey City, N.J.
Scrap Thatch

Photo-transfers on cloth, embroidery threads. Machine pieced and appliquéd, machine and hand embroidered, hand quilted.
91 in. by 65 in.

Comforter or discomforter? My work combines photography with traditional women's art forms and aims to create lush, seductive images out of the industrial landscape. My quilts contrast the conventional associations of stitched cloth—beauty, security and domesticity—with unlikely, provocative content and treat ugliness as though it were beautiful.

This work uses photographs of aluminum scrap piled in enormous pyramids at a commercial scrap metal recycling company in Jersey City.

AWARD OF EXCELLENCE

Catherine McConnell Stanton
Pittsburgh, Pa.
Peace Links at the End of the Rainbow

Photographic transfers on satin. Machine quilted. 44 in. by 80 in.

From a distance, the traditional friendship-chain pattern gives the illusion of a conventional quilt, which evokes sentiment. Yet upon closer viewing, you discover the photographic image of this pattern. The links provide a narrative of emotion in the wall of chains which speaks to the figure in the lower right corner.

Sue Benner
Dallas, Tex.
Tribute: Kuba Skirt Series II

Hand-dyed and commercial silk fabrics. Machine quilted and constructed. 85 in. by 36 in.

Emily Zopf
Portland, Ore.
Painted Bricks

Cotton and blended
fabrics screen printed
with Createx fabric
paints. Machine
pieced and machine
quilted.
41 in. by 53 in.

Painted Bricks was inspired by a wall that
had been painted many times over in
different colors. The paint had worn off in
areas to expose the layers of color and the
bare bricks underneath. The pattern of the
bricks and mortar was an underlying
constant to the changing patterns created by
the peeling paint.

In 1985 while visiting the Print and Textile
Study Room of the Dallas Museum of Art,
I viewed two raffia skirts made by the Kuba
people of Zaire. I was completely taken by
these exquisite textiles. More recently I came
upon these Kuba skirts on public display at
the museum. Seeing them again inspired
this new series of work based on the overall
form of the skirts as well as the pattern of
the appliqué.

THE HEART ASKS PLEASURE FIRST   AND THEN TO GO TO SLEEP
AND THEN EXCUSE FROM PAIN   AND THEN IF IT SHOULD BE
AND THEN THOSE LITTLE ANODYNES   THE WILL OF ITS INQUISITOR
THAT DEADEN SUFFERING   THE LIBERTY TO DIE.   EMILY DICKINSON

MA   MA

How do you like
your steak, Patty?

Thick and red,
Daddy!

IMPOSITION   Autenrieth '92

Patricia Autenreith
Washington, D.C.
Imposition

Cotton, blended and
found fabrics
(handkerchief).
Machine pieced,
direct and reverse
appliquéd, surface
designed with fabric
crayon, rubbings,
rubber stamps, copy
transfer and Ink-O-
Dye. Hand
embroidered and
hand quilted.
42 in. by 54 in.

It has taken me years to be able to juggle all
the elements that attract me in a single
work. It helps to work in an improvisational
way. My subject matter is memory, good
and bad. My intent is, well, to relieve myself
of various states of mind, to understand
them and in this way experience moments
of authenticity.

Wendy C. Huhn
Dexter, Ore.
Georgia, Frida, Mary and Me

Commercial cottons, fabric paints, photo transfers, beads and found objects. Machine pieced, hand and machine quilted, appliquéd. 33 in. by 43 in.

This is a self portrait. Georgia O'Keefe and Frida Kahlo are inspirations for me. I have always been a closet Catholic, hence the Virgin Mary. As a child, I was envious that Catholics wore hats on Sunday and ate fish on Friday. The dancing girls are me—in my many faces.

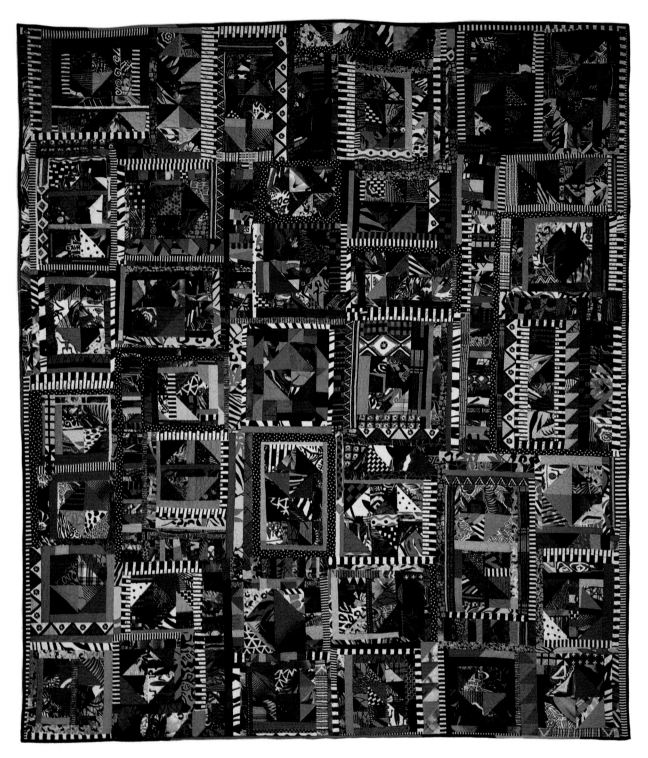

Ruth B. Smalley
Houston, Tex.
Rules Broken:
Running Rampant

Cotton fabrics.
Machine pieced and
machine quilted.
76 in. by 86 in.

Rules Broken: Running Rampant is an
improvisational play on traditional and
nontraditional blocks with an Afro twist.
Each piece was cut spontaneously by eye
and placed next to the preceding piece
totally from inspiration of the moment and
the thrill of seeing colors against each other
to form a cohesive design.

Esther Parkhurst
Los Angeles, Calif.
Scrapezoids

Cotton and blended
fabrics. Machine
pieced and hand
quilted.
47 in. by 47 in.

I have begun to loosen up my designs and
become a bit playful with the overall
composition. I enjoy simply composing with
many arbitrary pieces of fabric as if I were

painting. Black and white fabrics and their
contrast with vivid areas of solid colors
seem to dominate my current work.

Nancy Halpern
Natick, Mass.
Quarry

Hand-dyed and
commercial fabrics.
Hand and machine
pieced, hand
appliquéd and hand
quilted.
70 in. by 53 in.

The seaport where I was born was
constructed in large part from giant blocks
of granite ferried 200 miles south from a
quarry such as this. Now abandoned, old
tools share cracks with reclaiming trees, and
the carved ledges appear as an inverted city
made of air and imagination.

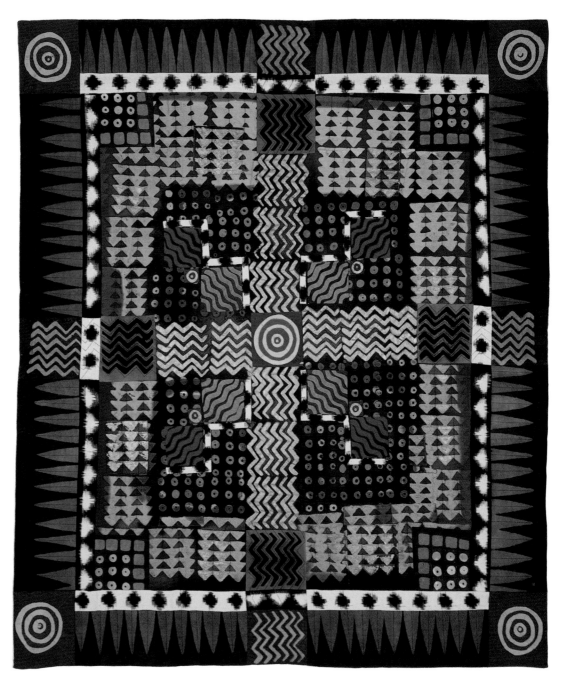

Ann M. Adams
San Antonio, Tex.
Blocked Energy

Block-printed, wax-resist and fiber-reactive dyes on cotton, discharge and metallic fabric paint, some Indian Ikat cottons. Machine pieced and machine quilted.
48 in. by 57 in.

This quilt was not planned, but rather something I let happen. Playing with dyes and printing blocks, I began to see a great amount of energy. This work isn't about energy that is blocked, as the title suggests, but about energy flowing through my printing blocks.

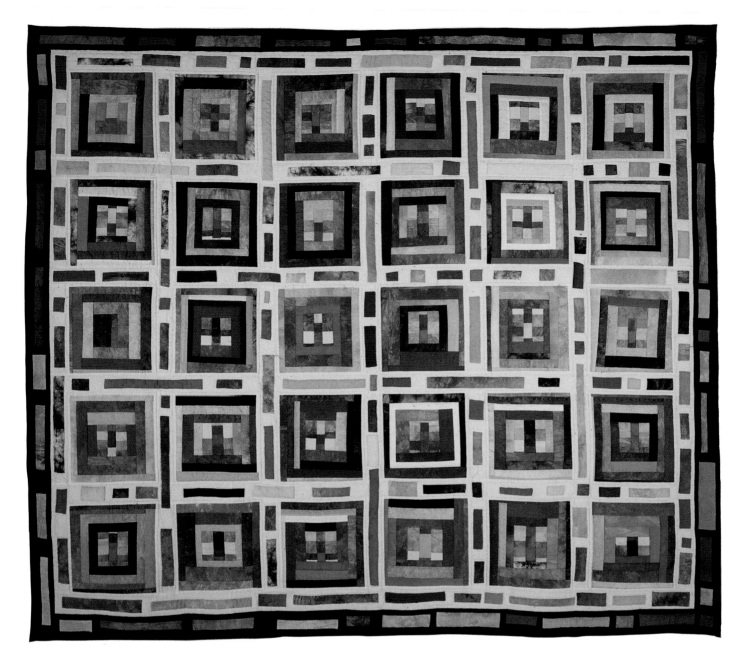

Joyce E. Seagram
Toronto, Ontario, Canada
Story Time

Cotton fabrics hand dyed by the artist and a Japanese quilt maker in Tokyo. Machine pieced by the artist and hand quilted by Edna Kopek.
66 in. by 57 in.

I think each of the 32 blocks in this quilt is telling a story. I remembered the nightly ritual with my four children of telling a story in an atmosphere of warmth, cleanliness, safety and love. Our imaginations would soar in high, happy and sad adventures. *Story Time* is a reminder of the fun, imagination and adventure in a child's happy bed.

Nancy Taylor
Pleasanton, Calif.
View from the Balcony

Commercial cotton and hand-printed fabrics by Ann Adams. Machine pieced, hand appliquéd, and machine embroidered by the artist. Hand quilted by Margaret Vantine. 69 in. by 86 in.

In *View from the Balcony,* the viewer looks out between two columns that frame the landscape below. There appears to be a large courtyard in the foreground, with architectural elements in the background; it is unclear whether this scene is an ancient location or a civilization of the future. In the middle ground a mysterious creature floats by. Are we intruders in his land, or has he entered our reality?

Anne Woringer
Paris, France
Quetzalcoatl

Cotton and silk
fabrics. Machine
pieced and hand
quilted.
42 in. by 42 in.

I once watched a television interview with
Claude Lévi-Strauss, the great ethnologist.
He spoke about some primitive objects he
really loved. Among the terrific masks was a
wonderful bunch of precious feathers with a
magic meaning. I immediately tried to
create a quilt that would evoke the strange
amulet. The title *Quetzalcoatl* arose alone—it
was the Mexican god "Feathered Snake."

Janet Shore
El Cerrito, Calif.
Cockeyed Optimist

Cotton fabrics.
Machine pieced,
machine appliquéd
and machine quilted.
47 in. by 41 in.

I have been a quilt maker for 20 years and
have taken hundreds of classes during that
time. After years of measuring carefully
and trying to sew exactly, I went in a
different direction when I made this piece.
By working spontaneously and limiting
myself to fabrics in my collection, I created
crooked log-cabin blocks. What fun it was to
"go with it!"

About the Jurors

Elizabeth A. Busch, Bangor, Maine. Busch holds a Bachelor of Fine Arts degree in painting and art education from the Rhode Island School of Design. For 20 years she worked as an architectural designer and also administered Maine's Percent for Art Program, which is responsible for placement of art in public buildings.

Busch has done several large-scale public commissions throughout the United States and has lectured and taught extensively throughout the United States and Canada. Her quilts have been exhibited in museums and galleries worldwide.

Michael W. Monroe, Reston, Va. Curator-in-Charge of the Renwick Gallery of the National Museum of American Art, Smithsonian Institution, Monroe has been associated with the gallery since 1974. He holds a Bachelor's degree from the University of Wisconsin and a Master of Fine Arts degree from Cranbrook Academy of Art. He taught design classes while director of the Fine Arts Gallery of the State University of New York, Oneonta.

Since coming to the Renwick, Monroe has organized exhibitions of contemporary American crafts. He has served as juror for many national and regional craft and art exhibitions. Monroe also lectures on themes and issues of contemporary American crafts.

Judi Warren, Maumee, Ohio. Warren holds a Bachelor's degree in art education from Eastern Michigan University and a Master of Fine Arts degree in textiles and printmaking from Bowling Green State University in Ohio.

Warren's work has appeared in numerous national and international publications and is included in several corporate collections. Her quilts also have been selected for dozens of juried and invitational exhibitions.

Warren is frequently in demand as a teacher and lecturer and has offered workshops in the United States, Canada, Switzerland and Japan.

Jurors' Statement

We believe that the cause and quality of contemporary quilt making is best advanced when each quilter creates his or her own original statement. For that reason, the single most important element that we three jurors looked for in a quilt is an innovative vocabulary of images that resulted in an individual style. This originality emerges from a unique interior vision in combination with a learned and controlled responsiveness to the materials.

In addition to looking for original vision and superb execution, we looked for quilts with a strong, fresh sense of design. All of the works in this Quilt National are excellent examples of how quilt makers transform color and texture into dynamic patterns that provide new visual experiences.

Ellen Oppenheimer's compelling and complex *Neon Maze,* winner of the Domini McCarthy Memorial Award, is a stunning example of design by a maker who simultaneously joins historical patterning traditions while dynamically overturning those same traditions. In sharp contrast to Oppenheimer's raucous and jazzy colors is Jan Myers-Newbury's Best-of-Show quilt, *Birch Eyes.* Limiting her palette to black and white, Myers-Newbury achieves a sense of awesome solitude in her pictorial representation of a stand of birch trees. *Birch Eyes* celebrates the restraint and subtle elegance that can be achieved without color.

Several quilters created designs using multi-layered patterns that when superimposed or entwined with geometric grids produced intricate visual puzzles. The use of words as image—sometimes bold and political, sometimes delicate and poetic—intrigued many entrants. A number of quilt makers delighted in creating an allover pattern using text as texture.

While several entries reflected a strong continuation of variations on traditional geometric patterns, others emphasized the free-flowing and organic shapes that are possible in the craft of quilting. Still others chose the narrative as their vehicle of expression.

An encouraging sign was the number of quilts that included non-fabric materials in their construction. Especially promising were several artists whose handling of diverse and often disparate materials with restraint represented a new level of maturity and sophistication. The most successful quilts incorporating mixed media are those where the makers used materials in support of their ideas as opposed to exploiting the purely seductive qualities often inherent in unusual materials. A strong example of this is Arturo Alonzo Sandoval's *Lady Liberty/Babylon II.* Winner of this year's Award for Most Innovative Use of the Medium, Sandoval uses high-tech photo-imaging techniques, Cibachrome photos, acetate transparencies, netting, paint, webbing and colored threads to produce a graphic image that creates a unified, powerful statement on nuclear war, terrorism and government corruption.

We were heartened by the number of quilts that revealed more skillful and sophisticated use of machine embroidery techniques. Quilters are utilizing the potential of machines to build multiple layers of threads and achieve rich, dense passages of shimmering color. Additionally, many artists adroitly used the machine as a drawing tool. Several quilters have taken pleasure in the expressive potential of loose threads by including the raw edges of unraveling fabric and untied threads to counteract their otherwise rigid geometric compositions.

In general we found that the materials selected by the quilters have become subtle, sophisticated and increasingly more personal. It was apparent that more and more quilters are creating their own patterned fabrics, thus allowing more control and expressiveness over their creations. This development, coupled with a trend to restrict the amount of artificial fabrics used in quilts, is one that we enthusiastically applaud.

Scrap Thatch by Merrill Mason, winner of this year's Award of Excellence, represents a mature example of a work that uses the technical aspects of photo transfer to support the content of the maker's visual statement, not just as a gimmick. The subject matter of Mason's quilt, scraps of metal in a junk yard, perfectly matches the technique of quilt making—the piecing together of fabric scraps. Her fabric construction is the perfect marriage of idea, technique and content.

We avoided including quilts that closely mimicked the ideas and techniques of well-known workshop presenters. We hope that quilters continue learning new approaches. But more important, we want to see quilters enlarge upon those new methods by taking risks with their newly acquired vision and create a highly personal format.

This year—the Year of American Craft 1993   is an especially exciting yearto have been invited to be jurors for Quilt National. This year-long celebration affirms the value of the hand by acknowledging craftsmanship as an important part of art. It is gratifying to know that the art and craft of quilt making will be strongly represented by this exhibition of remarkable quilts.

We, the jurors, would like to thank Emilie Ezell, Executive Director of the Dairy Barn Cultural Arts Center, and Hilary Fletcher, Quilt National Project Director, and her team of efficient and enthusiastic volunteers. We are honored to have had this opportunity to be rewarded so richly with the visual delights of this eighth Dairy Barn Quilt National. As we move into the final decade of the millennium, we believe that individual quilt makers will continue to express themselves in ways that are exciting and yet unimaginable today.

—*Elizabeth A. Busch*
—*Michael W. Monroe*
—*Judi Warren*

About the Dairy Barn

T he Dairy Barn Cultural Arts Center, a unique arts facility located in the Appalachian foothills of southeastern Ohio, has been showcasing the finest regional, national and international arts since 1978.

Harriet and Ora Anderson, long-time champions of the arts, worked with others in the community to establish a cultural arts center in a soon-to-be-demolished dairy barn just minutes from Ohio University and the center of Athens. Through their efforts, the historic building was saved, and the Dairy Barn Southeastern Ohio Cultural Arts Center, a non-profit corporation, was born.

The Dairy Barn, listed on the National Register of Historic Places, is now a state-of-the-art, handicapped-accessible facility that features a 7,000 square-foot gallery.

The Dairy Barn Cultural Arts Center is the site of festivals, juried international art exhibitions, educational programs and activities for all ages. To the international arts community, the Dairy Barn is best known for exhibitions and touring exhibits such as Quilt National, The Illustrator's Art: A World of Children's Books, the Neo-Iconography of T. F. Chen, and BasketWeave.

The Dairy Barn is supported by admissions, memberships, corporate sponsorships, grants and donations. The staff is assisted by a large corps of volunteers who donate thousands of hours annually.

Show Itinerary

The complete collection will be on display in Athens, Ohio at the Dairy Barn Cultural Arts Center from May 29 to September 6, 1993.

Following the exhibition in Athens, portions of the collection will travel to other sites through 1995. At press time, the bookings below had been confirmed. For information about the show's complete itinerary, call the Dairy Barn Cultural Arts Center at (614) 592-4981.

Houston, Texas
International Quilt Festival
George Brown Convention Center
October 28 to October 31, 1993

St. Louis, Missouri
Show sponsored by the Women's Self Help Center, site to be announced.
October 1 to November 1, 1993

Wilmington, Delaware
Delaware Art Museum
December 10, 1993 to February 6, 1994

Atlanta, Georgia
Quilts Across America
Castlegate Hotel & Conference Center
February 11 to February 13, 1994

Carson, California
University Art Gallery
CSU Dominguez Hills
March 22 to April 26, 1994

Wichita Falls, Texas
Wichita Falls Museum and Art Center
June 12 to August 7, 1994

Winnipeg, Manitoba, Canada
Winnipeg Art Gallery
June 25 to August 7, 1994

Bloomingdale, Illinois
Bloomingdale Park District
September 10 to October 22, 1994

Mt. Vernon, Illinois
Mitchell Museum
June 25 to October 28, 1994

Peoria, Illinois
Quilts Across America
Peoria Civic Center
September 30 to October 2, 1994

Bellevue, Washington
Quilts Across America at Meydenbauer Center
November 11 to November 13, 1994

Bellevue, Washington
Bellevue Art Museum
January 13 to March 3, 1995

Pine Bluff, Arkansas
Southeast Arkansas Arts & Sciences Center
October 2 to October 27, 1995

Index of Artists

Editor: Hilary Morrow Fletcher
Designer: Deborah Fillion
Layout Artist: Robert Olah
Photographer: Brian Blauser
Copy/Production Editor: Pam Purrone

Typeface: Palatino
Paper: Silverado, 80 lb., neutral pH
Printer: Arcata Graphics, Kingsport, Tennessee